MW00810817

Citizens of Ordinary Time

by Benjamin Goluboff and Mark Luebbers

Crossroads Poetry Series
Three Fires Confederacy
Waawiiyaatanong ✦ Windsor, ON

First Edition. June 2023

Library and Archives Canada Cataloguing in Publication

Title: Citizens of ordinary time / by Benjamin Goluboff and Mark Luebbers.
Names: Goluboff, Benjamin, author. | Luebbers, Mark, 1958- author.
Description: First edition. | Series statement: Crossroads poetry series
Identifiers: Canadiana (print) 20230457649
            Canadiana (ebook) 20230457681
            ISBN 9781988214504 (softcover)
            ISBN 9781988214511 (EPUB)
Classification: LCC PS3607.O525 C58 2023 | DDC 811/.6—dc23

Book cover design: D.A. Lockhart
Cover Image: Bill Evans, 1964 by Seppo Heinonen (public domain)
Book design/layout: D.A. Lockhart

Published in the United States of America and Canada by

 Urban Farmhouse Press
www.urbanfarmhousepress.ca

The Crossroads Poetry Series is a line of books that showcases established and emerging poetic voices from across North America. The books in this series represent what the editors at UFP believe to be some of the strongest voices in both American and Canadian poetics.

Printed in Adobe Garamond Pro

For Catherine and Stephanie

Contents

Introduction

Speculative biographical poetry is narrative verse in which imaginary events are written into the life of a historically verifiable person. These are poems that make music from the data of our subjects' lives even as they amend, extend, or redirect the narrative of those lives. In dialogue with the factual record, but unfaithful to it when it suits them, speculative biographical poems ply a devious course among the particulars of a life.

Maurice Manning's poems about Abraham Lincoln (*Railsplitter*, 2019) are a beautiful example of the sort of thing we're trying to do and an illustration of how spec-bio poems have feet in different worlds. The voice in Manning's "Reading Burns as a Boy below a Tree" is Lincoln's speaking from the afterlife about history, his own and the nation's, and about poetry as discipline and mystery. The poem's particulars involve the boy Lincoln at home near Pigeon Creek reading Robert Burns in the shade of a tree. The boy is lying head to trunk and as the day passes and his reading deepens, Lincoln shifts position to stay within the moving shadow of the tree. The boy and the book become the hands of a clock measuring time together; Manning's poem, rooted in facts about Lincoln's life but growing beyond them, becomes a meditation about poetry as a force within and outside of time.

Robert Penn Warren's *Audubon: A Vision* (1969) was certainly part of the apparatus Manning brought to his Lincoln poems. The seven movements of this narrative poem both derive and depart from the given facts of Audubon's life as they engage with big questions about nationhood, environment, and ambition. Centrally, Warren's Audubon is about the mystery of identity: Audubon in flight from his illegitimate origins, Audubon as stand-in for the lost Dauphin, Audubon as one in a long line of American reinventors of the self. Warren's Audubon stood:

> At dusk, in the street of the raw settlement, and saw
> The first lamp lit behind a window, and did not know
> What he was. Thought: I do not know my own name.

We have chosen the subjects of this collection in part for their associates, networks, and acquaintances. We like Forrest Gump figures, Jamesian ficelles. The illusion that the past was a small world is certainly the result of what psychologists call confirmation bias. On the other hand it is true that Emerson walked in the woods with Jones Very, that Mary Lou Williams let Dizzy and Monk and the others use her apartment. We love Florine Stettheimer as *saloniere* no less than as painter; we love Iris Tree for the many artists in whose gaze her beauty was refracted no less than for her beauty itself, her wit, and her weirdness.

We write about lives in the arts as a way to write about the arts themselves, to exercise an ekphrastic impulse, and to test a variety of propositions about the dyer's hand and what it works in. We like oddballs and iconoclasts, obsessives and outsiders: Bill Evans at war with himself and at war with the conventions of his music, Robert Frank afoot with his vision and haunted by an idea of America.

We write about Larry Waters and James Longstreet because we are attracted to taboo subjects. Longstreet is taboo not only because he fought to defend slavery but because of how his life has been misremembered by Americans sympathetic to the toxic Lost Cause myth of the Civil War. Waters is taboo because of the dark magic of his terrible story.

Some of these subjects we chose because they gave us the opportunity to write about great works of art. Gerda Taro's photographs are peerless renderings of a pitiless war. One hundred years out, Jacob Epstein's bronze of Iris Tree as goddess of war still fascinates, implicates us. The imaginary lyrics to one of Bill Evans's best-loved standards tell about the dark resonance of possessive love.

At one time we considered writing a suite of spec-bio poems about Joseph Cornell, who lived a rare and strange life while making his "shadow boxes": assemblages of found objects, finely chosen to create unique and often ambiguous visual moments. The Cornell Box has a family resemblance to our poems, we think. Cornell would have made a great subject for us, but we discovered that we were late to the dance because Charles Simic had brilliantly exhausted the subject in 1992 (*Dime-store Alchemy*).

Our collaboration began in 2017 when Mark found an article by Ben on the blog of the late and much-missed Chicago literary journal Bird's Thumb entitled "Confessions of an Anti-Confessional Poet." Mark felt that he'd found his poetic Doppelganger when he read, "Many of my poems have been biographical narratives, which I've written in suites or sequences . . . These poems combine facts about these people with a good deal of invented detail and circumstance." At that time Mark had been working on a series of poems about imaginary moments in the lives of artists, capturing them when their aesthetic or ethical principles were tested or changed - people like Charlie Harper, Paul Laurence Dunbar, Alexander Calder, and Laura Ingalls Wilder.

Even though we'd never met and lived far apart (in Cincinnati and Chicago respectively) Mark wrote to Ben and we decided to team up for a Beaumont-and-Fletcher, Becker-and-Fagen, Rogers-and-Hart-style collaboration by correspondence. Since then we've traded ideas for potential subjects and built these suites with little intention (until recently) of producing a book. Perhaps there is some voyeurism in what we do, as well as some fanboyism, but we've learned a lot in writing this and maybe that makes up for all our peeping and perseverating over these dead people.

The main thing we want to say about collaborative writing is that it is enormous fun. We make these poems in a spirit of play and would compare our collaboration to one of those improvised games of childhood whose rules are variable and evolving and in which there is no final winner. One of us will "serve" up a first draft for the other to return, followed by a volley, and the resulting rally lasts until we agree (often telepathically) that the poem is done.

We would like to claim that these poems begin with facts about our subjects and end with truths, but like most worthwhile games, a lot goes on without much adult supervision. It has been delightful to venture into the lives of these fascinating people, and we are grateful to them. Our subjects lived lives even more colorful than the ones we're wearing today, and we've had the bad manners to rummage through their closets and make ourselves costumes to try on. We acknowledge the intrusion and apologize if we have not put everything back where we found it.

Iris Tree

Iris Beerbohm Tree (1897-1968) was photographed by Man Ray, filmed by Fellini, cast in bronze by Jacob Epstein, and was the subject of oil paintings by Modigliani, Augustus John, and others. The child of renowned actors, Iris grew up surrounded by explorers, authors, caricaturists, composers, and librettists. She studied as a painter and became model and muse for artists in the Bloomsbury Group. In the years after World War I she published two volumes of poetry, and in the 1920s became a fixture in the avant garde social life of Paris. During this time she also began an acting career and came to New York after leaving her first husband, the American artist Curtis Moffat. She soon married Friedrich von Lebedur, an Austrian Count, and with him traveled in California before moving back to Europe and performing with the Chekhov Theatre Studio. She worked in Hollywood in the 1950's, but lived her final years in relative poverty and anonymity after returning to England.

Photo credits: public domain

She Chooses A Role, 1913

W.S. Gilbert was a fixture at Father's table, where he made, it was said, advances to Mother that were as cleverly expressed as they were improper in design. Ellen Terry presided at the Christmas theatricals Father produced for the children each winter, her beauty refined and enlarged in old age. And Father was knighted in 1909 during the run of *Twelfth Night* at His Majesty's. Playing Malvolio, he spoke of how greatness comes, and the people rose and silenced him with their applause.

The question for a child growing up in these theaters was, always and emphatically, who to be, and young Iris addressed herself to this question with deep misgivings, as it seemed that all of the roles had been previously assigned. So at age 16 in a second-class carriage from Wolverhampton, Iris cut off nine inches of her hair (her luminous, red-gold, Pre-Raphaelite hair) and left it, a strange bouquet, on her seat when she emerged at Paddington Station.

A Bust of Iris Tree by Jacob Epstein, 1915

In winter the first airships
slid black over Great Yarmouth.
By spring, the big guns at Ypres
fired shells filled with chlorine gas.
Jacob cast Iris as a goddess of weapons:
impassive face terse and ancient
lichen skin of roughened verdigris
decayed eyes just averted
as if she'd witnessed
every last slaughter
caused by our inventions.
Her neck thick, inured to holding
the polished mass of her bullet crown
which reflects its surroundings
in an arc of perfect distortion.
Mouth too long clogged
by enormities remembered
to speak of those coming:
a failed sentinel against
war's genius and industry.

She Smokes Hashish, 1916

That was the summer at Bognor, back in the dunes, when Iris at nineteen held in Nancy Manners' Kirby Grips a tiny smoldering ember of hashish rolled in a strip of *The Telegraph* (Father called it *The Tory-graph*) inhaled deeply and waited, as Nancy vomited on the sand, for what would come.

Some aspirant boy had bought it for them from an Algerian at the docks and Iris was expecting arabesques, but what came, along with the sense that her peripheral vision had contracted, was a series of *aperçus*.

First, that unlike sexual experience, which was a wanting that could result in a having, aesthetic experience was a wanting of what never could be had.

Also, that the odds against living the dreary conventional life of her time, place, and class were so laughably, implausibly bad, that her own escape must be treasured—consciously, actively, treasured—for the singularity it was.

Further, that time was inescapably subjective, that growing up was a growing away, and that her hair was certainly her best feature.

These and a good lot of rubbish that only made sense at the time.

**A General Practitioner from New Jersey Encounters
Iris Tree and Nancy Cunard, Paris, 1924**

Bill saw them
together twice:
at *Le Dome*
then *La Rotonde*,
early hours—draped
reptilian in chairs
or banquettes.

Once
dancing together
beneath halos
of smoke and absinthe
faces masked
with white powder
mouths rouged.

Hollow
beautiful youth,
their dance
an alethic artifice
a surrealist
composition
it seemed to Bill
for these
disordered times.

The Dr. described
this condition
in a letter to Demuth
where he called
the girls
"unassailable,"
compared them
to the vector
of an advancing
contagion.

A Brief Guide to Posing by Iris Beerbohm Tree

Becoming a provocation begins
by arranging the bones behind the throat.
The cervical vertebrae must align lightly
so the spine becomes an arching staircase
descending as the scapulae drape
from the shoulders like needless wings.

Positioning the torso becomes then
little more than permitting each segment
to assume a delicate irony with the hips
flowing thus into the legs hidden beneath.

Each arm should evoke small dramas.
In the tilted wrist, the arch of a finger,
a delicate pathos must sit, a rarefied disdain
or a shade of the languor after passion.

As for the head, a gentle magnetism
should call the tip of the chin
toward the peak of the shoulder.
The mandible and cheek, vaguely hollow,
will be drawn taut in a dissolute geometry.

The lips will indicate a recent word
of droll indifference, a wry allusion.
The eyes will present a balance
of curiosity and insolence with the lids
awning over the pupils' suggestive softness.

The techniques described above may be applied
to any circumstance, and will make you
the cynosure, muse or provocation
of garden, club or atelier.

With practice you may come to know yourself
through your likenesses in various renderings
And you may be confident that neither artist
nor audience will ever see the same model twice.

1968: She Approaches the End

Late in January Iris walked between
the flats of friends in London
who had provided her
with charitable bivouacs
since her car, which served also
as her wardrobe and library
had been stolen. She passed
a storefront window where
behind her own image reflected
in the glass, she saw displayed
the latest color tellies
who called to her with shifting
images of studio and stage.
A bitter evening
and Iris was long and deeply cold
but she stopped for a moment
to watch a mute Hughie Green
tease up his contestant
on *Double Your Money.*
Iris saw that the woman
full of electric optimism
had been winning for some time
and was poised to reach £16,384.
She watched the faces
of both host and contestant
tighten with concentration.
Although she could not hear
the crucial question, Iris imagined
herself on stage, answering
after a long and ironic pause
with an enigmatic *non-sequitur*
something Wildean, something
Father might have said, or Aldous
(that dear man) a surrealist aphorism
to befuddle the audience into silence.
And before walking offstage she would
conclude with Hughie's own signature line:
"And I mean that most sincerely."

Bill Evans

Bill Evans (1929-1980), a major innovator of jazz piano, combined classical training and intuitive touch to make music that was both cerebral and poignant. Despite struggles with addiction and depression, Evans influenced or collaborated with many of the essential figures in modern jazz. Already a veteran working musician as a teenager, Evans left home in New Jersey to study classical music and composition in Louisiana, then traveled with trios and bands before a stint in the Army. Afterwards he worked and studied in New York and was influenced by the theories of George Russell. Evans was a crucial member of Mile Davis' sextet in the late 1950's before he formed his own seminal trio, which included drummer Paul Motian and bassist Scott La Faro, who died in a car accident in 1961. Evans continued to play and record important music with major figures in jazz throughout the 1960's and 1970's, but addictions, first to heroin and later to cocaine, as well as attendant health, legal, and financial problems ultimately took their toll.

photo credit: Comunicon.es "Bill Evans Trio - Live at the Penhouse Seattle 1966" source: Flickr

He Reads George Russell's *The Lydian Chromatic Concept of Tonal Organization*, 1954

Gil Evans hipped Bill to the Concept
and Bill read the whole thing at a sitting
then read it through again
shaking with caffeine and fatigue
wordless as the words took hold in him.

The morning broke Copernican.
How would one speak
who could one be
in this world made new?

The Lydian mode
like the white-note scale
starting from F
with a sharpened fourth
but also unlike
as inhabiting a realm
where like and unlike
stammered into silence.

What held the system together
Russell asserted
in a metaphor
that Bill accepted
with perfect conviction
was "tonal gravity"
a force linking mode to mode
scale to scale
through the duration
—Russell called it the "mass"—
of a given root tone.

The hair on Bill's arms stood erect
the light in the room was altered.

Here was escape from the 32 bars
from the Broadway song structure
in which jazz had been held a captive
all these years, as if behind iron,
as if in a cell.

Later Bill would write
about the Concept
comparing it
(another metaphor)
to the lines of a Japanese
calligrapher.

What he saw now
was a labyrinth of pathways
branching vertical
and horizontal
leading to freedom.

Thirtieth Street Studios, 3/2/59

This is not some tuxedo gig in the Village
and the stand is wide but not quite level.
Under blue light he waves his horn slow.
"We don't need no whitey opinions
Moe. You so damn square," he says.
But I'm tight. I'm the irony in every set.

My head bent right-angle I never see
my fingers arch over the thin space
between each key. I will phrase
from way in here and ease us down
add soft pedal, eat crow to Jimmy's
smooth brushes, while Miles holds
his mute so we can each have our say.

He Solos Alone

"... I have always preferred playing without an audience."
—Bill Evans

The changes are temporal
but he experiences them as space
as wall meets wall
as the chord resolves
enclosing him in this room
with the instrument.

Here he presses toward a stillness
he never can achieve
fails always to answer
the instrument's question.

Why He Got Addicted to Junk

Wasn't about living down Plainfield, N.J.
and all that square noise with his daddy.

Wasn't to be down with the colored musicians,
or that nonsense about how it give a player touch.

Philly Joe Jones was not the Prince of Darkness
and Bill was not out there playing Faust.

Bill Evans got addicted to junk
for none of these reasons.

Bill Evans got addicted to junk
because junk is delightful.

Junk is post-bop, modal.
Junk is delightful.

Waltz for Debbie (Alternate Take)

If I could keep the room sweet
could keep you from the weary
work of being grown, keep

the window lit somehow
with sun, sin somewhere
else and silent. Secure there

then you could hear just
the music I would play to set
you to a tender dance.

Before an audience of dolls
I would make you permanent
unaware that the gold in the air

is nothing but dust hanging in light
and the soft floor you spin on
nothing but a clown's closing palm.

After the Death of Scott La Faro

Past midnight the Dodge rolled over
and left the curved pavement
of Route 20 near Flint
in the Finger Lakes.
The sweet double bass
in the back seat was crushed
but not caught in the fire.

Back in the city there was a low long
time off through the autumn:
a numb space in which loss
could improvise
but then the piano
slid over again into the first bars
of that Gershwin tune
as if on its own.

Arrested for Heroin Possession at JFK

"What Kind of Fool Am I?"

Standing beside the shining baggage claim
the pianist wishes for evaporation, as opposed
to flight, since he has just come to ground.

'72: early in the decade, but late for absolution.
The carousel is empty, still, yet humming in key:
stainless planes linked in sequence, an endless scale.

Waiting for the valise holding his fix to reach his hand
the marshals are static outside the automatic doors
in sunlight and heat. This is for them a minor affair.

He has tried again to be honest with his lovers.
He has repaid the money to his friends.
The carpet looks so cool, so broad and smooth

he would like to reach down and feel it with his fingers.
He sees his reflection, jacketed and tied, in the glass
and the half-note difference between black and white

forms a space in his mind where he rests for a count.
Then the switch is turned on and the carousel keys slide.
Somewhere inside a beat begins and so he must play.

Robert Frank

Robert Frank (1924-2019), was a Swiss photographer and avant-garde film-maker best known for his book *The Americans,* which documented his travels around the U.S. in 1955. His raw and disorderly black and white photographs of ordinary people in mundane settings captured the melancholy, ironies, and paradoxes of American life. His work was at first dismissed as ugly and even subversive, but was eventually championed by writers and artists of the Beat movement, and subsequently celebrated for its honesty and spontaneity. In the 1960s, Frank moved away from photography and made films with and about such figures as Jack Kerouac, Allen Ginsberg, George Segal, and The Rolling Stones.

Photo credits: public domain

Fourth of July, Jay, New York, 1954, **Gelatin Silver Print.**

An American flag
hangs vertically from a line
or fixture unseen above the frame.
Giant, diaphanous, patched and rent
and of an obsolete edition, it reaches down
to a foot or two above the summer grass
holds the entire weight of the humid gray air
and consumes this little park in a town upstate
where celebrant families have gathered
to shroud themselves in another day
of independence.

26

Yom Kippur – East River, New York City, 1955, Gelatin Silver Print.

Five men in fedoras stand with their backs to the camera
while a boy in a *kippah* shows
his right profile against the Brooklyn shore.
Glimpses of the river appear
in the spaces between the figures.

Invisible and emphatic in the photograph:
the empty field where European Jewry used to stand.
Because all the figures in the picture
are facing away from us
(except for the boy in the *kippah*,
who is looking at something
the others are not)
we are made to occupy that emptiness,
are fixed in it like ghosts
watching the living move on.

Statistics Taken From *Canal Street – New Orleans*, 1955

The sidewalk is crowded, the time is midday.

The weather is warm, the light slightly hazed.

The background is the darkly shaded window of a department store or other business. In it, the buildings across the street are dimly reflected.

There are 23 people in the frame, visible only above the waist.

10 are male and 7 are female.

5 are of undetermined gender because part of them is invisible.

6 are black and 9 are white.

5 have features or are positioned in a way that makes their race unclear.

3 are children younger than, say, 10.

4 are past middle age, while 9 are adults between the ages of, say, 20 and 50.

4 of the women and 1 girl are wearing dresses, 2 of which are printed with flowers.

4 of the men are wearing suits.

3 people are wearing glasses, 1 of whom is a black woman.

1 of the children is a white girl who is looking over the back of a man who is wearing a suit and is carrying her above his waist.

1 of the children is black, but since their face is not visible, the gender of this child cannot be determined.

4 of the men are wearing hats, and 1 of these men is black.

The race of the other 3 men cannot be determined.

2 people are wearing clothing printed with stripes.

1 is an older white woman, the other is a young white man, and both of them are wearing an expression of self-absorption.

7 are facing right, and 10 are facing left.

1 young white man is the only person looking into the camera, and he does so with an expression of guarded suspicion.

2 people are smiling, but not at each other.

1 black person of indeterminate gender is facing left and is looking at someone in front of them with guarded suspicion.

4 hands are visible.

1 is the right hand of an otherwise invisible black man, which appears to be about to gently touch the left cheek of a white boy whose expression cannot be determined.

1 is the left hand of an older woman of indeterminate race who is facing left and is wearing a dress printed with flowers.

She may be shaking the hand of someone of indeterminate race and gender who is otherwise invisible.

She may also be about to gently touch the back of the head of a black child whose gender and expression are not visible, but this is not clear.

Robert Frank Meets Jack Kerouac: Two Sides

NB: There are at least two accounts in print of how Robert Frank and Jack Kerouac met. We made poems out of both versions of the meeting.

Avenue A, New York City, Autumn 1957

The party had spilled out
on to the sidewalk
when this little owlish guy
filled his cup from the jug of Dago Red
Jack was passing around and
Jack was aware the guy
had his eyes on him.

A breeze came down the block
all "Autumn-in-New-York" and
Jack turns up his collar and
says to the guy:
"It's not a fit night out
for man nor beast." And

the little owlish guy (and
in this the little owlish guy
is revealed to Jack
as a prestidigitator
impresario angel
sent to him from above)
he pantomimes the door
blowing open and
snowflakes flying
into Jack's face and
everybody busts out laughing.

So they talk about Fields,
and they talk about Chaplin and
Jack is totally in love with the guy,
wants to make him his
faithful Indian companion.

When he learns that the guy
is a photographer
on a Guggenheim year
making a portfolio of American scenes
Jack explains to the guy
about photography
about how it intervenes, dad.

The writer's always chasing lost time
but the photographer intervenes
-- between tick and
tock, between diddy and
bop -- the photographer
precedes and prevents us.

They talked about
the little towns on Route 66 and
Jack improvised a while on
how lone and lorn
out there was and
he tried unsuccessfully to remember
the second half of Allen's line
about visionary Indian angels.

Frank sent him the prints
a couple days later and
Jack wrote the Introduction
in two hours, including the time
he spent crushing on
the Miami elevator girl and
staring sad and lost
at the photo of the St. Francis statue
greeting the dawn in L.A.

At the Viking Offices

The walls were wood and stainless
held in by the tall glass looking
out over the avenues. Fall
and Joyce remembers seeing
from her desk the man step
from the elevator, wearing sandals
holding close under his arms
a big square black portfolio
and saying he needed to see Jack.
Joyce remembers telling him
Jack was in a meeting
and wondering who this guy was
and what the editors would think
they in all their buttoned-up
patrician squareness
they who mostly saw Jack
as their own trained bear
dressed and acting as he did
as if he had just stumbled in wild
from up there in the north woods.
What would they think when they
saw this new strange guy
with his face wearied
and eyes which clearly
had seen too much, so long
away from the sheen of the city
instead lost on the roads
between the empty fields
and in the wet streets
of the bruised mill towns?
So Joyce remembers Jack
walked out in front of the crew cuts
and saw Frank's pictures
spread from the folio
and right away he knew
the eyes behind the camera
had seen the same flags and factories
and cars and storefronts and faces
and cares that he had seen:

the vast homely country
waiting to be loved and lamented
and unforgotten, knew that the pictures
he had been trying to make with his words
had here been made into pictures

knew that here was another crazy immigrant

who could see the necessity of a new idea
and that the suits behind him needed them
both more than they could know
and so he said so.

Coffee Shop, *Railway Station – Indianapolis*, 1957, Gelatin Silver Print

The subject of the photograph is the light
that makes the photograph possible:
how it descends from fluorescent tubes
above the head of the waitress
gathers in bright lozenges
on the aluminum lockers behind her
holds in luminous embrace each slice of pie
in the mirrored case to her left.
Like a bright haze the light softens contrast
and obscures detail. It occupies the dark skin
of the waitress like a mask.

On a Photograph of Robert Frank with Joyce Johnson at the Naropa Institute, Boulder Colorado, 1982

They might call it disembodied, Frank would have been thinking,
but the Institute was institutional, with its minions and minders,
its designated wise men, its mission to codify and preserve, its tendency,
like the Protestants, to reach back through time to a point of origin
or primitive church. And Johnson would have been thinking: funny how culture
moves from the fringes to the center, from a constellation of eccentrics
to a movement, an aesthetic, an institute. She'd called Jack a big bag of
wind once, outside some bar some drunken Village night; funny to think
the wind was blowing here.

Discovering the Limitations of the F-Stop

And in those days a figure
for the national character
was abroad in the land.

Begotten by the Cold War
upon the Turner thesis
christened by Bob Jones
it had become a principle
in the landscape Frank traveled
in the heat shimmer on the interstate slab
in the exhaust leaving winter chimneys.

The figure was the silent assumption
behind the jukebox in the candy store
or at the pumps of a gas station, among
the pickup cowboys and the bikers.

Frank was both an artist and no fool
so he understood the figure to be real
even if it wasn't true.
It hung unphotographable
between his lens and the Americans
danced upon the vanishing point
where road kissed sky.

And it almost did him harm, the figure,
a time or two in the South.

Florine Stettheimer

Florine Stettheimer (1871-1944) was a painter, costume and set designer for opera and ballet, a poet, and avant garde socialite who hosted, along with her two sisters, many of the great names of modernism at salons and parties during the years between the World Wars. Her wealthy father left the family when she was young, but her mother had substantial means, so Florine was enrolled in a German private school and later trained at the Art Students League in New York. Along with her mother and sisters, she traveled throughout Europe in the years leading up to World War I, attending lectures by Henri Bergson and performances by Nijinski and Ballets Russes. The Stettheimers settled in New York in 1914, but as Jews they were excluded from many social circles. However, led by Florine, they gathered together American artists and writers, along with many who had fled Europe, and formed a circle of modernist luminaries. As a painter, Florine is noted for a style which incorporates elements of impressionism, folk art, modernism, and surrealism, but she is not beholden to any movement. Her work is both deeply feminist and highly personal.

Photo credits: public domain

She Hosts a Party in Her Studio, 1917

The fainting couch
the potted palm
the light as it is distributed
on the Cellophane drapes;
these are simulacra
for signatures and essences
I will never see or know.

The same with the people, alas:
Van Vechten curving into his chair
Georgia looking like a phrase turned perfectly
dear Marcel with a *Gitane* in his face.
These are cut-outs arranged conventionally
in the blinking eye of the present
in the ornate clock of the mind
whose every gilded second
is gilded onto the past.

Everyone is laughing, except Marcel
who wants to appear immune to the joke
but whatever Picabia has said to amuse us
has already gone into the past.
All the particulars slide into the past:
each cut flower in the Lalique set
its times of bud and bloom
the liquors and glassware
before and after the mixing
and serving and laughter.
These can only be preserved
by hand and craft.

I will set up shop by the river,
please my fool wish to frame
some instances of its flow.
I will subscribe to that fiction;
I will insist on that luxury.
I have the means and in at least one sense
of that abysmal word, the time.

Stettie's Garden

Like Delphi or Cusco, Stettie's little garden
was built upon the center of the world.
We may imagine it this night near midsummer 1932,
asleep in Bryant Park, asleep behind the lions
of the New York Public Library, 42nd and 6th.

The artist is away now and the garden is empty
except for its little share of Manhattan no-dark
and the June aromas of linden flower and the city bus.

Her garden's plan, an express rejection
of the British picturesque style,
involves modernist play
upon classic French tropes
and blooms in a narrow palette
of whites and pinks that her friends
know to read as an irony.

Wherever she may be tonight
Stettie is thinking about the garden.
Her *mise en scene* for many an interior drama,
the garden often fosters, for Stettie,
a meditation on the difficulty for the artist
of control over her materials.

Materials are refractory in every medium
(froward children, dogs straining on leash)
but for the gardener materials present
various special challenges.
They cannot be asked to hold the mirror
up to nature, being nature themselves.
Because they are not words
they cannot draw through themselves
chains of imagery from the mind.
And because they are not images
they cannot draw through themselves
the corresponding chains of words.

For these reasons the topiary frame
next to which she stands
in an undated photograph
was a great consolation to Stettie.
On its simple conical form she has disciplined
the unruly vine of the Moonflower (*Ipomoea alba*)
which will not bloom for her this summer
because of a disparity in the photoperiod
between Manhattan and its native Peru.

Otherwise the plants here are thriving.
Stettie knows a cunning little Catskills nursery
and had them install two summers ago
a half cubic yard of forest loam black as pitch
so for all its rectilinear precision
the place now has a potent fertility
and if fauns and nymphs were to appear
anywhere in midtown, it would be here.

New York/Liberty, Oil on Canvas, 1918-1919

The dreadnoughts with guns erect
face each other in the blank harbor.
The guns of the flagship are trained on us.

Flags on each bowsprit and crow's nest
fly right and a Great National Leader
stands alone on the flying bridge.

Behind the fleet the city stands at attention
watched over by ships of the air.

Virile towers rise from the pink skin
of the avenues in the Financial District
topped by flags that all fly left.

Liberty Island is flooded
and Our Lady has lost her green patina
gained gilt and some weight
but still stands her vacant watch.

From the shoreline upriver the taut arms
of the bridges reach out but what they grasp
has been omitted.

The terminals of the Port Authority
gape like mouths half-submerged
singing an anthem in gargling harmony
that entrance to the tabernacle
is sealed with a myth.

She Exhibits at Knoedler, 1916

With all but a knowing wink
Mrs. Knoedler,
of Knoedler on Fifth,
explained to the gallery staff,
Myra and Bea,
(both of whom took classes at the League)
that the exhibit they were to dress
would be a "friends and family affair."

The young women understood
this meant a monied hobbyist
with associations in *le monde*
who might bring feathers
to the Knoedler nest
and they smiled indulgently at Mrs. K.

Bea and Myra amused each other
as they hung the canvases
to the hobbyist's specifications:
country gardens and city parlors
plump stylized figures
in crude perspective
and bright nursery-room palette.
"Matisse *manqué*," said Bea.
"Would-be primitive," Myra said.

Both gallerists, however,
considered the work of dressing
Mrs. K's big front room
as the artist's *boudoir*
to be lowering,
even somewhat indecent.
As they unrolled the rugs
arranged the daybed
covered the artist's vanity in lace
Myra and Bea felt they were made
accessory to a solicitation.

When the friends and family
showed up for the big night
the gallerinas found them to be
a perfectly humdrum group:
the cosseted rich
Manhattan provincials
so intent on one another
nobody looked at the art.
It was galling to think
they considered themselves
the *avant garde*.

Heat, Oil on Canvas, 1919

Each summer the city seethes
blooming with argument, odor
and infection, until maintaining
la vie artistique becomes a trial
and one escapes if one can.
We repair to anywhere pastoral then
even Bedford Hills will serve:
a rented house with garden
to effect the privileges of exile
to languish unburdened by guests
who suffer us to summon them hither.
In the green hours we perform our repose
perspiring in costume for our own audience
each on an equidistant throne, a set piece
composed on the stage of the lawn
our little pantheon plays under wilted trees
while the afternoon's confections
rest unsampled and spoiling.

Larry Walters

Larry Walters (1949-1993) had always dreamed of flying and enlisted in the Air Force during the Vietnam war, but was denied training as a pilot because of poor eyesight. After his tour of duty he returned home to California and worked as a truck driver. Larry became famous on July 2, 1982, when he tied several dozen helium-filled weather balloons to a Sears and Roebuck lawn chair and took a 45-minute flight over San Diego, rising to an altitude of 16,000 feet and eventually landing entangled in power lines on a suburban street in Long Beach. As his notoriety faded, he became increasingly religious, served as a volunteer ranger for the National Forest Service, and worked sporadically as a security guard. He eventually committed suicide by shooting himself in the heart while camping in the Angeles National Forest.

Photo credits: FLICKR: omnibus

Larry Walters Ascends: an Epistemology

When the tether was released
and the chair began to rise
there came an uncanny sense
of recurrence or confirmation
as if he now knew
somewhere deeper than knowing
that his childhood dreams
of flight were true
that he had known
without experience:
the lift, the lurch
in the pit of the stomach
as the ground fell away
and the horizons retreated
and retreated again
to reorganize the scale
of the given world.
He understood
as the balloons
pulled him upward
that there are
parts of the mind
where knowledge
precedes experience
parts of the mind
where we have flown before
we've left the ground.

He Makes a Simile

From fifteen thousand feet
the Los Angeles River,
captive in its concrete aqueduct,
looked like the slot
in a model-car raceway
or a crease scored ruler-straight
down the gray urban page.

Larry fixed on the river in its box
as he drifted east with the prevailing wind
and the river, on a drift of seeming, moved west.
He reflected that most of us are like the L.A. river:
making our shallow way between walls of convention,
arriving -- if we have force enough to arrive --
at a foregone conclusion. Larry was so pleased
with the conceit and with his authorship of it,
he forgot for a moment that he had escaped.

He Relinquishes His Means of Descent

In principle, shooting the balloons
gave the endeavor at least
some semblance of control.
Each one punctured would keep him
bound reasonably to the earth.
Otherwise, he would be wholly subject
to the whims of atmosphere.

In truth the whole contrivance
expressed his long-held hope
for a loss of control, a negligence
of bounds, at least for a time.

The gun, while it proved effective
pulling him down a little
from the blue cold three miles up
soon left his mind
which was understandably
in a haze of rapture.

Still he was surprised
that he could not see a loss
when it clinked off the chair's arm
and spiraled prettily
toward the streets of Long Beach.
He sent with it a sincere hope
that it would do no harm
but as he watched it fall
he was also wondering why
he had overlooked
the need to tie it on.

On a Photograph of Larry Walters After Landing in Long Beach, California

A ranch house front yard:
jacaranda shades the early afternoon
over a police cruiser, a Malibu
parked at the curb.
The officers stand on the sidewalk
discussing the incident with the neighbors
and another press photographer
who carries equipment bags
across each shoulder.
One cop has a clipboard
which holds the standard form
to diagram the vectors of travel
for parties involved
in common traffic accidents.

Walters walks by in the foreground
apparently unnoticed.
From the chair under his arm
the plastic water jugs hang
empty of their ballast
and the umbilical remains
of the heavy tethers
drag along the pavement.
His face is tired, expressionless,
elation having left barely a residue.
Soon he will give the chair away
to a local kid, and arrive home
in San Pedro empty-handed.
But right now he looks ahead
having flown, having survived
having avoided, today at least
prosecution, and still carrying
his burden down the street.

He is Remanded to the Heaven of Birds

His suicide had not disqualified him
as he might have supposed.
Perhaps he had grown devout enough
in the years preceding
to mitigate this sin.
Rather it was decided
upon his arrival and application
that the cheap wings
issued to neophytes
– Icarian toys really –
would be sort of a dis
and the designated paradise
for creatures of flight would be
to one of his inclinations
simply a better fit.

In any of the various heavens
transformation sort of
comes with the deal.
Once the paperwork was done
and he had moved in
Larry was given the features
of those species he admired
in order to start his eternal avian life:
the hawk's eyes, of course
the resourcefulness of the crow
the buzzard's broad wings
for spending timelessness aloft
even, yes, the stubbornness
of a woodpecker, and so on.

Granted, when all this fettling up was done
he was not the handsomest gander
in the flock. But then
he had been pretty plain
as a person – nondescript, humble.
So, unlike the peacocks
or the birds of paradise,

cardinals, or what have you
vanity wasn't a problem.
He was good with the look
as long as this new apparatus
could keep him up there.

Gerda Taro and Robert Capa

Gerda Taro (Gerta Pohorylle, 1910-1937) and Robert Capa (Endre Fried-
man, 1913-1954) were photographers, collaborators, and lovers who together
photographed combat and civilian life during the Spanish Civil War. Having
fled political repression and anti-semitism in their homelands of Germany and
Hungary as teenagers, they met in Paris in 1934, where Friedman taught Pohor-
ylle the craft of photography. Together they adopted the alias of Robert Capa
in order to fool skeptical editors who would not publish the work of a female
photojournalist. As supporters of the anti-fascist Republican cause, they began
making forays into Spain in 1936, and their work found international acclaim.
After changing her own name, Taro's work became independently recognized,
but she was killed during the Socialists' retreat from the city of Brunete. Though
the authenticity of some of his most famous photographs has since been ques-
tioned, Capa went on to further renown as a photographer in World War II, and
afterwards in conflicts in China and Israel. He founded Magnum Photos with
Henri Cartier-Bresson, and became a friend and photographer of writers and
filmmakers including Ernest Hemingway, John Steinbeck, Truman Capote, and
John Huston. He was killed by a landmine while on assignment in Indochina.

Photo credits: public domain

Robert Capa Made in Paris

In bed they pass the Leica
back and forth.
No film just for the form
and frame of the thing:
Gerta's clavicles,
bare above the drawn-up sheet,
the curve at the base of Endre's spine.
She is so small he fears
that he will crush her
but she takes his weight
with a strength that seems
more than her own.

Together they are a composition
of taut surfaces in spilled light.
Together they are exposed;
they burn and they dodge.
They make love in a language
that is native to neither
for they are stateless in Paris
(this their joke)
having come to Europe's head
from its hooves,
or in Gerta's case
(less one generation)
its filthy matted tail.

Another joke
in those innocent days
was about the secular Jew.
If a Jew, not secular,
the lovers laughed;
if secular, not a Jew.
They made jokes,
Gerta and Endre,
whoopie they made
prodigiously
and they made

– each to each
the muse and mentor –
many photographs.

They made as well
a nom de travail
an alibi man,
over whose variable signature
they would send their work
into the world.
Robert would be good
for the American market
Gerta said
and Capa the "shark"
would do, said she
and they had to be a he,
said Gerta, and he
would be Robert Capa.

All Partisans, Especially the Little Ones, Must Wear Hats
(Two Photographs by Gerda Taro)

1.

During the siege of Madrid
an orphan boy is eating soup.
The mess table is high
which allows for the delicate
resting of his chin
on the bowl's wide white rim.
The clean spoon, levered by his fingers
is level just below his eyes
which regard us with the dark clarity
of a stoic.
Thanks to the sponsors of the picture
he has been clothed
in a new shirt and crowned
with a regimental sidecap,
tassel lying left, which cups his head
gently like a patient hand
of providence and conscription.

2.

Among the barricades and bricks
in the center of Barcelona
a boy poses proudly
in the rolled shirt sleeves
and pleated trousers
of the working man.
His legs are planted with bravado
atop a fallen sandbag, and his thumb
rests under the strap
of a small knapsack on his shoulder.
His mien tells us he imagines
he belongs to the struggle
and that he is capable of any charge
because he wears a toy cap
of glossy paper, shaped like a soldier's
fixed under his chin with a string
and bearing the initials
of the anarchist militia.

She Photographs Refugees at Malaga, 1937

The Moscow trials began
almost a year before Taro photographed
the families fleeing the fallen city
in shambling lines of crying children
and goats and donkey carts and cooking pots
and stained laundry and broken furniture;
or camped and huddling in scarred churches
and makeshift tents and the ruins of homes like their own.
People everywhere on the left
were defecting from Stalin.
There were many issues,
Taro understood,
from agriculture to the woman question,
where the party line was all wet.
And she had just witnessed
the limitations of the Soviet military intervention
in the spectacular Republican defeat here:
cadres marching sheepishly off to prison or firing squad,
feeble artillery left broken, the dead, equine and human,
lined up by the Fascists for display.
And yet, making images of one more migrant mother,
Taro, herself the child of refugees,
knew the Communists had been right,
at least for a while,
about one thing:
nationality is a lie.

She is Mortally Injured Near Madrid, August 26, 1937

Messerschmitts had been above all day
and the clownish retreat on the ground
had sucked the glory out of what had seemed
at least a beautiful defeat.

As Brunete fell, she rode, deflated,
on the running boards
of General Walter's staff car,
there being wounded in the seats.
Her dismay was perhaps not so much
in the loss of the city or in the dying
of the Republican cause.
Regardless of the outcome, she knew by now,
Vu or *Regards* would want the pictures.

More it was that the pictures themselves
had become for her mere reportage:
soldiers beneath the sign on a market,
two more carrying a burdened litter,
and looking up at passing shells or planes,
a burning truck in the street.
These, once developed, she feared
would prove to be pedestrian
without even a shade
of the ecstatic ether of war
which was everywhere she looked,
but somehow just beyond her lens.

When the tank, a T-26,
Russian and unreliable
like the General,
came clattering in reverse
from the rubble
and struck the car broadside,
she had been wondering
if there was such a thing
as too close.

Alberto Giacometti, Commissioned to Make Gerda Taro's Memorial

Giacometti received the commission
from Louis Aragon, then at the height
of his influence with the Party,
who, from the sculptor's point of view,
was still trapped in the cage of Surrealism.
Something between manner and mannerism
was how Giacometti saw the movement
now that the fever and spasm
of his own time with that harlot were done.
Juxtaposition, inconsequence, a whiff
of supercilious irony, *et voila...*
It looked silly even on the French.

When he began negotiations with Aragon
for Taro's memorial (Poor lady,
she was in love with war, they say),
Giacometti had already begun
his turn to the figurative.
The sculptor's meditations
on the figure were long and hectic:
he thought of the figure as alive
in a million narratives of singularity,
multiplicity, and type, of the figure
as transaction between
trans-historical principles
of liberty and constraint,
of the figure as aleatory,
hermeneutic,
as a dwindling down
to a vanishing
point.

Giacometti was in deep ontological waters
with the figurative when Aragon's check
for the first installment arrived
(And just where did the Communists
find this kind of money?)
but Aragon's banal requirements

64

for the granite brought him briefly back
to 1937 Paris:
By unanimous vote of the subcommittee,
the falcon avatar of Horus, Egyptian river god,
would adorn the tomb
of our fallen comrade
as a symbol of continuity and rebirth.
Giacometti smiled at the pompous language
and at the intellectual dishonesty
of the Frenchman's conceit.
Surely this was old wine in new bottles.

Be true, he would reprove
the gentlemen of the Party,
be true to your well-advertised materialism.

But Giacometti reproved no one,
cashed the checks, and made the falcon
which sits, inconsequently,
on a corner of Taro's plinth
at Pere Lachaise
as if it had just set down there
and closed wings.
The bird's profile is hieroglyphic
and its body, beak to tail, is elongated,
as if the falcon were subject
to longitudinal pressure
from within, as if something inside it
were struggling to get out.

Reviewing Photographs of Gerda Taro, Robert Capa Grieves

In the months after her death
people kept sending him photographs of Gerda:
her parents – which was agonizing –
friends and colleagues, stringers and fellow-travelers,
Peggy Guggenheim, whom Capa had not met,
but who evidently wanted to assist in his grief.

These he would review as a craftsman,
assessing their technical values and compositional points,
even as he consumed them
as the lover consumes the image of his beloved,
even as, reporter of his times, he glossed each
for the narrative content
it carried to and from the world of events.

In one (heart-stopping, taken from below)
she is sheltering behind an embankment
with a Republican *suboficial*,
her expression, though partially hidden,
is rapt as she looks for the German plane.
The *suboficial* has a carbine in his hands
and a sword on his belt;
Gerda appears to be wearing pumps.

In another, with which Capa tormented himself,
she is lifting her skirt to show a little thigh.
Then there was the portrait dear Fred Stein made
of the two of them at the *Dome*
the time they had the joke
about the Soviet generals
as characters from Sholem Aleichem
and Sholem Asch.

Going over his archive,
and over it again,
Capa would spend hours
absent from himself,
abstracted in a kind of time

that was not ordinary time,
even though, like ordinary time,
it inflicted and incurred
but differed because our ordinary time
will get you somewhere at last.
But the time that presided
over Gerda's pictures
was an eddy or back-wash,
a stagnant pool.

Here the photographer
was trapped for seven years,
as the thirties became the forties,
as other women came in and out of the frame
until, not long before the Normandy landings,
Capa was able to put the pictures away
and become a citizen of ordinary time again.

American Writer Ernest Hemingway With His Son Gregory. Sun Valley, Idaho, USA, 1941: A Photograph by Robert Capa

All day they've been shooting
upland birds, and in this pause
the logging bridge across
the Big Wood River lies
in repose under the filtered sun
of a leafless season, warm
enough for Papa's rolled sleeves
and the unbooted bare feet
of the Huck of a boy
who nestles in Papa's shadow
head against the raw log rail.

Two guns also recline:
the lighter single lying apart
the bigger over-under cradled
in the crook of the boy's sleepy arm.
The barrels of both point out
over the river's patient surface.

Father and son too
look out over the water.
Father must be speaking
for speaking is what fathers do
at such times, and the words
we know, even from a father
known for powerful words
would be less powerful to the son
for what they mean
than for having been spoken.

Although the exposure
captures everything in the scene
reaching from the solid timbers
of the bridge, to brushy islands
past the shoulders of hills
to mountains lying low
on the horizon

and though the western air
is clearer than it will ever be
again, there is no sign
or evidence at all
that any game has been killed
or of how the day will end.

Cornell Capa Says Kaddish For Robert Capa, Amawalk Friends Meeting House, Yorktown Heights, N.Y., 1954

The artist rests at Amawalk among the Quaker dead.
Time is made of granite there, time is like a stone.
The ancient Aramaic prayer is what his brother said.

His brother came to Amawalk to stand among the dead
and sing the words of praise among the silent Quaker stones,
the prayer that intervenes among what's silent and what's said.

Some of our best Jews are Friends, the elders must have said.
The dead are a congregation. His brother came alone
to bless the artist resting there among the Quaker dead.

The Quaker dead at Amawalk have stones at every head.
To mark his time of mourning, alone but not alone,
the ancient Aramaic prayer is what his brother said,

when he came to Amawalk to speak among the dead.
Time is passing slowly there, time is like a stone.
The ancient Aramaic prayer is what his brother said
beside the artist resting there among the Quaker dead.

Jones Very

Jones Very (1813-1880) was an American scholar, poet, essayist, mystic, and clergyman, who became associated with the Transcendentalist movement. Very was born in Salem, Massachusetts, to unwed first cousins. His mother was a confirmed atheist, and his father was a sea-captain who took his young son on a two-year voyage to various ports around the world. As a teenager, Very distinguished himself as a scholar of Greek and Shakespeare, first as a student at Harvard and later as a lecturer there. He wrote acclaimed essays on Shakespeare and a series of extraordinary Shakespearean sonnets. In his twenties he became consumed by religious passion, and his fervor resulted in dismissal from Harvard and commitment to the McLean Asylum. After his release he was supported by a group of Transcendentalists led by Ralph Waldo Emerson and Margaret Fuller, and for them he performed religious rites and sermons, during which he claimed to be the Messiah. He later cast off this role, asserting that his time as prophet had expired, and he returned to Salem, where he lived his remaining years as a recluse under the care of his sister.

Photo credits: public domain

Age Ten, He Encounters Bioluminescence in the Equatorial Atlantic

The schooner under Father's hand
made fair passage south by Trinidad
under a night without clouds or moon.
Some time after one bell
in his apprentice middle watch
the boy was struck curious
then amazed, as beyond the deck
the milky roiled sea ignited green
all around and beneath the craft
and he watched the paint of light
spread almost to the horizon.

His hold on the moment began to slip
as a sense grew that he was reading
a godly primer given for his direction.
The luminous waves and wake
gripped his eyes against his will.
He heard himself whisper cries in fright.
The creaking and rumble
of rigging and sails,
the lowing of the hull
moving through the water,
became an oracular chorus
then a single voice
that squalled his name,
as if bidding him to dire labor
or to sacrifice.

He pulled his gaze up
between fore and main
and was calmed for a breath
by the southern constellations,
by their stillness and gravity,
though they were to him nameless.
Then he was drawn again into awe
by the myriad bodies of the firmament
their immeasurable sweep and dimension
and he knew each light was falling

on him in sentient witness.
The lights calling below
and those watching above
pressed onto him
an unbearable exposure,
a helplessness in which he trembled
and squeezed shut his eyes to escape,
only to find the glare
residing there too, and he knew
this would not subside.

The Mad Poet of Concord Reflects upon his Family Name

My name is an intensifier:
a part of speech
amphibious and supple
that attaches
both to adjective and adverb,
and sometimes
-- a painful coupling
or lexical miscegenation –
to nouns,
both common
and proper,
as in "I am very Jones."
Very deepens,
elevates, enhances.
The intensifier magnifies,
as Romish angels
by their song
are said to magnify
the glory
of our Lord.
The intensifier
is transparent,
refers its being
to the quality it enlarges.

And I would be
as very is,
(I would be verily,
I would.)
a selfless self
to magnify
the works
and will of God.
I would
by my witness,
I would
by my prayers
thus intensify,

and by
the reformed
sacraments
of our
New England church.
Thus my hope,
my hymn
and anthem, thus
– forgive the term –
my magnificat.
Like the intensifier,
too, it must be said,
I am quite alone.
I have no plural form.

Two Eagles Lead Him Beyond Himself

He was willing to concede
that in recent months
his lectures had swayed
from the stated curriculum.
Yet his students had been rapt
as he set down his Greek texts
to wax, vehement and off-hand,
on the small fontanelles of God's light
everywhere about them in the land.
Indeed they were even there
in the staid lecture room
where the students listened
and he implored the men,
just younger than he, to see,
to conjoin their intellect
with the holy spirit and rise
above mere classicism.

His dismissal was therefore
not surprising, not disheartening,
since he read in it another auspice
that he had been commissioned
by an authority beyond scripture
with the power and duty of a seer.

Under skies mottled with fall
Very walked about Concord,
where he had repaired
once released from the scrutiny
of the hospital and the University.
He had found here friends
of sympathetic ear and probing speech
who prodded and fanned his godly passion.
He shared their minds and parlors
and felt he was, for the time at least,
a chosen man in a place blessed.

North of the village the local rivers met
and above the Assabet he saw,
one afternoon, two eagles wheel.

This was not in itself a portent.
The black and white birds
fished these waters in season.
But in his ecstasy Very saw
that these were a recurrence
of the same pair sent long ago
by Zeus as surveyors
to fly from the earth's opposing ends,
so the god might divine, at the point
of their convergence, the *axis mundi*.

Very saw no sacred stone on the muddy bank
as the birds held with the wind
downstream toward the Merrimack.
But his vision was undeterred,
the bridge in his mind was crossed,
he stepped finally beyond himself,
past doctrine, past liturgy
and divined he was the new logos
standing before the new oracle.
He would be its sole and holy guardian
and a clarion in his prophecy.

He Acknowledges the Pull of the Foreign Faith

…and in my prayers it is like a crosswind
drives athwart my purpose
or a current sets across the course I've set.
In my walks and ways, my idle hours,
a stranger to myself, I feel a pulling force
as the compass is pulled from true to less true.

Like the world were polished wood
and had a grain and that grain ran toward Rome,
or if not Rome, then Oxford, where Newman,
one has read, fed the young men who sat as his feet
with richer fare than our reformed traditions serve.

These thoughts are poison, well I know:
treason to self and treason to church.
That they abide unbidden suggests, I fear,
a second self behind the self, a self in thrall
to unclean spirits and the Scarlet Woman.

I would turn from the Scarlet Woman,
blot out her name and stop my ears,
but I would also, to my shame,
hold her by the haunches,
put my face between her breasts.

He Intends His Retreat Into the Wilderness

If I must feed
I will take only
the raw violet
painted columbine
windflower
and wild rose
wandering the field.
I will take only honey
from the stinging hive
in the locust's hollow.
I will take only
the smallest creatures
in carapace or scales
dispel my hunger
with the bitter
and the biting
brought to my hand
without gun or snare
or brought to my feet
by provident ravens.
I will not taint
my penury with alms
or company
though I will walk
in my exalted state
as sleepless as the moon
behind the farms
above the towns
persecuted by the air
but drinking the rain
or from the brook
open-mouthed
clothed only in a mantle
woven from nettles
and serrated grasses
pulled from the fen.
And when I have
anointed fully myself

with suffering
I will return to you
to display the litany
on my wasted skin:
weeping sores, cuts
red afflictions, patched filth
and you will have no will
to turn away, but only
obligation, from fear
chagrin, or pity
to concede
my earned sanctity
to accept
my blessing.

He Identifies the Rules of the Sonnet with the Laws of Nature

Turn and counter-turn and stand
are lyric laws ordained by Man.
They are like the laws that rule every tribe,
to turn us from incest or bar suicide.
They further the ode as it reaches forth hands
to conjure a muse that it cannot command.
But the laws of the sonnet are fixéd, divine,
like the laws of mortality, being, and time.
Eight calls to six; six answers eight
as tides to the moon must gravitate.
The sonnet's rules are laws of force
that keep Earth balanced on its course.
Eight calls to six; six answers eight,
lest integers disintegrate.

James Longstreet

General James Longstreet (1821-1904) was one of the most successful Confederate generals of the Civil War, but became a pariah in the South when he joined the Republican party during Reconstruction. Born into a family of plantation and slave owners in South Carolina, Longstreet was educated at West Point and served in the Mexican-American war with his friend Ulysses S. Grant. After he resigned from the Army and joined the Confederacy in 1861, Longstreet became a trusted subordinate of General Robert E. Lee, and played a crucial role in numerous Confederate victories. After the war Longstreet settled in New Orleans and tried his hand at several business ventures, but found himself engaged in the conflicts of Reconstruction. He published letters arguing for reunion and reconciliation, and thus became anathema to many Southerners, who eventually blamed him for the loss of the war. Nonetheless he was recruited to defend New Orleans from White League insurrectionists by leading an integrated militia, but was captured at the ill-fated Battle of Liberty Place. He later was converted to Catholicism, served as a U.S. Marshall, and as U.S. Ambassador to the Ottoman Empire. In ill health during his final years, Longstreet again tried to retire to a farm in Georgia and spent five years writing his memoirs in order to answer his critics, only to see the farm destroyed by fire.

Photo credits: public domain

On an Equestrian Monument Never Erected to General James Longstreet

The granite plinth bears a modest plate, which reads:
"Unhorsed at the Battle of Liberty Place, September 14, 1874."
The outsized bronze decorated with guano
commemorates the moment Reconstruction ended,
which was the moment when the New Orleans militia
of citizens and freed slaves fled his command
across Jackson Square and into the *Vieux Carré*.

The great steed is foreshortened, rearing, eyes rolling, nostrils flared.
The heavy rider is forever tipping from the saddle,
hands freed of the reins and of his saber.
His left boot is out of stirrup, near level with the pommel.
His billowing coat shows the opening the minie ball made.
The brimmed hat also dismounts as the long beard strays skyward
and on his face lies a scowl of permanent dismay
as he is pulled to the ground by the invisible hands
of the Crescent City White League and other sons of the Lost Cause.

The Woods He Came From

As a nation we claim to honor
certain traditions of woodcraft:
navigation by map and compass,
the eye that reads track,
spoor, and weather sign,
marksmanship with its honorable
conventions of thrift and compassion.

From these, at a thousand firesides,
we have made a figure of virtue:
the virtue that pays the bearer on demand,
that gives title when we drive the Canaanite
from his hills and groves,
striking out his name, root and branch.

The figure is expansive and attaches to many:
Copperhead, Minuteman, Seminole-Killer.
We look into the mirror
of our disappearing woods
to see ourselves as pioneers.

The woods he came from,
Georgia's Piedmont,
were in the 1830s a fertile matrix,
fons et origo for this figure and its traditions—
especially in those upland valleys
the locals call coves.

Here, playing truant
in the company
of an antique fowling piece
handed down from his Uncle Augustus,
Longstreet, beneath a canopy
of Basswood and Tulip Poplar,
became himself.

The boy became an adept of the place,
found his way by the stars

and by memory, knew the resort
of the timid hellbender
and where, each fall,
to dig the forked ginseng.

A party to all the secrets of the cove,
James met one August morning
a coyote pup emerging
from a recess in the laurel.
The size of a house-cat,
her eyes full of tender inquiry,
the unwary pup stepped
right up to the boy who,
hesitating not a moment,
took its head off with a single shot.

James Longstreet and Ulysses S. Grant Audition for the Role of Desdemona, Corpus Christi, Texas, 1845.

Longstreet always called Grant Sam,
all the boys did, all the way back to West Point,
but not all the boys called Longstreet Pete:
that was for family and, sometimes, for Sam.

Sam was twenty-three and Pete twenty-four,
piss-ant second lieutenants,
when they followed old Zach Taylor to Texas,
there to establish a just and equitable border
with the Mexicans, who had some misguided notions
about where the true boundary lay.

Picture the two of them on a muddy parade ground
by the piss-colored Nueces River,
in smelling distance of a dank little town
with a Papist name whose only feature,
besides a rank and inflaming local drink,
was a battalion of mestizo whores.

Now both of these amenities
exercised a powerful magnetism
upon the rank and file of Taylor's army—
so much so that enforcing curfew,
patrolling the street of seedy cantinas,
and ceaselessly drilling the men
became the chief responsibility
of the junior officers who,
according to the conventions
of their time and service,
were expected to be immune
to the temptations that drew the enlisted men.

To further occupy the corps until the spring
when they would march south,
Taylor tasked Captain John Bankhead Magruder,
a Virginian who had opinions about this sort of thing,
with building a theater and organizing

a program of amateur theatricals.

Magruder duly established a joint stock company
that would charge admission to the 800-seat theater
his company built of Palo Verde
and good old Texas Post Oak
on Taylor's parade ground,
there to perform a repertory of plays
by William Shakespeare,
whom certain wags under Magruder's command
came to call the Swan of Nueces.

Othello was the first of the plays
to go up in Magruder's folly,
and we might number it
among the moving accidents
of flood and field
occasioned by the Mexican war
that James Longstreet and Ulysses Grant
both auditioned for the role of Desdemona.

As ever, when young people rehearse plays together,
the script stole into the lieutenants' daily speech,
engendering shibboleth and double-speak,
adorning ordinary usages
with the nimbus of theatricality.
As he got into his cot in the tent the boys shared
Sam would say: "The tyrant custom, most grave senators,
hath made the flinty and steel couch of war
my thrice driven bed of down."
Or to convene, of an evening,
the junior officers' poker game,
Pete might say, "Get weapons, ho,
and raise some special officers of night."

Inevitably, with the fleshpots
of the little papist town
never far from their minds,
Othello moved both boys
to thoughts about the beast with two backs.

As a southerner Pete had more
experience in this field than Sam,
but not so much that Desdemona
didn't get into his mind too:
imagining what the Moor did to her
and she to the Moor:
the ewe and the ram,
the ram and the ewe.

Pete's edition said "tupping"
where Sam's had "topping"
and the two verbs hung between
the tent-poles all night,
hung in the boys' inflamed imaginations,
a rhyme and not a rhyme,
a team unevenly yoked,
suggestive of couplings and socketings
the thought of which left Pete and Sam
impaled all night, each upon his cot.

All agreed that Sam
made the prettier Desdemona
but that Pete had the more imposing
stage presence and a more
natural way with a speech.
In the end, however, Pete
was disqualified as being more than a head
taller than Magruder's choice for Othello:
Theodoric Porter, the scion of a distinguished
military family, who would die gruesomely
at the Battle of Matamoros,
some weeks after the show closed.

Pete did not resent his friend's success in the role,
harbored no thought that he
might have made the better Desdemona.
And while it would have been impracticable,
as well as unmanly, to give Sam flowers
on closing night, Pete gave his friend,
as he came flushed from a final turn
on Magruder's folly, a bootjack, a cigar,

and a shaving brush bound up,
bouquet-style, in a strip of rawhide.

Taylor marched south when the winter broke,
and while there were some notable engagements
(Pete was shot through the thigh at Chapultepec
and passed the regimental flag
to Second Lieutenant George Pickett)
the Mexicans cannot be said to have made much of a show.

The two friends met just a handful of times after that.
Pete stood up at Sam's wedding in 1848,
then a chance reunion at a St. Louis transit depot
not long before Secession compelled
the friends to choose different sides.
Then once more at the courthouse at Appomattox,
where Sam offered his hand to the defeated Longstreet,
and proposed one more game of poker.

Pete thought of his friend often over the years,
saw him in the drifting smoke and muzzle flash
of many a contested field.
But the image that most often came to him
was Sam in the muslin and fright wig
that made him the black ram's ewe.

He Responds in Print to the Passage of the First Military Reconstruction Act, 1867

"The striking feature,
the one that people
should keep in view,
is that we are a
conquered people…
Recognizing this fact,
fairly and squarely,
there is but one course
left for wise men to pursue,
and that is to accept the terms
that are now offered
by the conquerors…
Let us accept the terms
as we are in duty
bound to do,
and if there is a lack
of good faith,
let it be upon others." [1]

[1] *New Orleans Times,* March 18 1867.

He is Constrained by the Economy of Reconstruction

During his years in New Orleans
Longstreet pursued several commercial ventures
including the sale of insurance
and membership in the city's cotton brokerage,
either of which, before the war,
might have brought him a comfortable return.

But the General,
who had known command
in a different world,
was too blunt and naïve
for the scarce and subtle business of those
post-war days, found his means reduced,
and wrote letters seeking
accommodation of his debts.
His penury, of course, remained
both private and a matter of degree,
since he was a man of modest habits.

He was discomfited, then,
each of the several times
there was a knock on the broad door
and the servant revealed the caller
to be a veteran of his Corps:
one who had fought at Antietam perhaps,
or Fredericksburg, and now
was seated before the General
threadbare and gamey
and bragging that he had
"just killed me a Yankee."
Even settled deeply as he was
in the good chair's horsehair cushions,
Longstreet recoiled as he recognized
the false boast to be coded beggary.

Still he would find for the man
a bag of food from the pantry
and walk with him to the hall.

But after setting him out
with farewell and exhortation
the General would turn
inward with dismay
at the frailty of the renewed Union
and apprehension
at the reckoning of his name.

Why He Joined the Party of Lincoln

Not because of any feeling
the General might have had for the freedmen.
(Except that if they was to have the vote
some of us ought to be in the tent there with them.)
More because he had been raised
to believe a deal was a deal.
You swap knives with a fellow one day,
you don't take yours back the next
because the fashion don't suit.

They had licked us fair and square he figured
licked us up one side and down the other
and there weren't no sense in acting
like it had come out some other way.
War is a promise, the General knew.

But there was another thing
that made him stand with the Republicans
when the shooting was over
and that was the ghosts.

Every commander's got them:
spooks and night-walkers
more than dreams and tall-tales,
less for damn-sure than the men they were
and they followed the General
like a bluetick follows scent.

There was a boy who lost his face at Knoxville
used to show up pretty regular
wherever the old man billeted.
Others too. But they all said one thing
to the General: No more war.

He Makes Confession to Father Abram Ryan, 1878

With what's left of the throat shot through
at the Wilderness, and by my own boys,
I whisper it again:
regret, Father, never contrition.
Regret that I chose the cause
that ran athwart of history,
that I studied so hard to further
the agency of Old Scratch in the world.

But no contrition. Like those ancient Hebrews,
Father, I was born to kill my brothers.
Loyalty to one clan equals betrayal of another.
That's how the sum comes out for me
and the proof is everywhere you look.
I read it in the newspaper every time
that damned Jubal Early makes
a speech somewhere.

And I will do no penance, Father.
That account is squared, I say:
my dead children, my farm burned,
my slandered name.

When you were sweet-talking me away
from the Episcopalians, Father,
you said there were no politics in this church
and I have forgiven you that lie.
Now, please, absolve me of my regrets.

He Writes his Memoirs

"It is well that war is so terrible. Otherwise we should grow too fond of it."
—Robert E. Lee

You would think
that when he sat down
in New Orleans
in 1890-something
to write his memoirs,
having lived far longer
than he ever supposed he might,
that General Longstreet fought
all the old battles once more:
marched once more
the barefoot marches,
ordered Pickett's division once more
into the Dantean field of fire
at Cemetery Ridge,
lived again what happened
at the Wilderness to his arm.

And in some measure this was true
but there at the roll-top desk
morning after morning
turning out those
Ciceronian periods
for whose elegance
he was indebted
to the instruction
years ago
of Uncle Augustus,
the General found himself
battling new adversaries.

Revisionism sought
at every chapter
to turn Longstreet's flank.
Self-aggrandizement
advanced to cut off
his lines of supply,

and like a battalion
of subtle sappers
harassing his columns,
Romance lay in ambush
to make him forget
that the horror
was merely horror.

He Attends Alumni Day, June 9, 1902

At the Centennial Exercises
commemorating the founding of West Point,
Longstreet, in morning coat and four-in-hand,
with the sash bearing his honors
heavy across his chest,
was among the dignitaries
on the dais behind President Roosevelt.

He was seated alongside Daniel Sickles
who had been a poor adversary
at the Peach Orchard on the Second Day.
Although they had reconciled years before,
Longstreet still believed the New Yorker
to be of low and immoderate character.

He was not in the Order of Address
but Longstreet was announced
to the assembly during the oration
of his former artillery chief, E.P. Alexander,
whose grand speech, like the ancient epics,
testified to the valor of the great southern soldiers
and proclaimed, as the humid afternoon wore on,
the noble exploits of each one in turn.

And following the utterance of Longstreet's name
in the cavern of Cullum Hall,
there was a prolonged and thunderous hurrah.

For years afterward, Sickles would tell his friends
that in the din, the Georgian had turned to him and asked,
"What are they cheering about?"

Mary Lou Williams

Mary Lou Williams (1910 - 1981) was a jazz pianist and composer whose career spanned all the eras of the music's evolution. As a child virtuoso in the 1920s she traveled the country in various blues and boogie-woogie bands. By the 1930s she was in demand as a player for big bands and jazz orchestras, and later became a central figure in the hard bop scene of the '40s as mentor to a generation of aspiring musicians in New York. Williams was famous in 1954 when she abruptly quit playing and converted to Roman Catholicism. Eventually she returned to music, collaborating with many jazz luminaries, composing and recording devotional pieces, and becoming one of the first professors of jazz as an artist-in-residence at Duke University.

Photo credits: public domain

Age Ten, She Plays for Afternoon Tea in Pittsburgh, 1920

The Mellons paid the fare for two,
plus Mary's standard fee, a dollar an hour
so her cousin could take her on the trolley —
the red 96 from East Liberty,
to the green 71 down Fifth, to Shadyside —
where they were admitted from the service gate
walked behind the walled garden with its fountain
and funny naked statues and went into the kitchen
where her cousin had to wait.

Old Sturzio had given her
a repertoire of fashionable classics,
had said Mary might mix
in some popular parlor songs.
And she played just fine
but was surprised and a little let down
to see, once the novelty of her gift wore off,
hosts and guests going back to balancing
their cups, their *petit fours,* and conversations.

And to be sure, the great and good
of Squirrel Hill had much to discuss
but an agreeable decorum required
the omission of several topics including
the end of the epidemic,
Mr. Wilson's League, socialist labor,
the rising prominence of the Klan,
Amendments 18 and 19,
and what to make of this little brown girl
in her Sunday white dress, white socks
and patent Mary Janes who,
though dwarfed by the massive Steinway
gleaming in the drawing room,
played as if it was her own and who smiled
a smile of fine bemusement
as if she was wondering:
would they stop talking
if she broke off in the middle

of "Moonlight Sonata"
and went hard into
Ma Rainey's "Crazy Blues?"

Fats Waller Throws Her Into the Air, 1925

Mary was playing
the theater circuit with Buzzin' Harris
in his "Hits and Bits" traveling revue.
Fifteen, her father sick,
she was glad to have the job
although alone and far from home.

By the time they got into New York,
playing Connie's Inn and The Lafayette,
some names had come to hear
"The Little Piano Girl"
and Duke had her sit in for a week
at the Hollywood Club.

Fats dropped in on a session
while Mary did her bit, striding through
"Tea for Two" or another show tune
and after: there he was
in acres of pinstripes
smelling of lavender and Luckies
smiling like she was his long-lost little sister.

This joy of his, this recognition,
irrepressible, of kindred presence,
was what caused her flight
as he launched her
from his hands under her arms
toward the lights
then in her descent
catching her there
and setting her down.

Abashed as she was when she landed
while Charlie Irvis, Sonny Greer,
all Duke's boys, laughed and clapped,
she realized that in that half moment,
freed from gravity, she had all the time

to see the expanse of the stage,
all the space in the empty club,
all of them looking up to her as she flew,
and she realized the prospect
as a confirmation.

Two Doors

1947

Whether she was home or not,
Mary kept the door to her place
on Hamilton Terrace unlocked --
not because she thought
Sugar Hill was safe,
or believed herself
to be protected.
It was just easier, in the end,
than getting up and running down
to let one of the young cats in,
or handing the keys to one of them
from wherever she was playing.

They came to Mary's place
for different reasons:
advice about a chart
or a prima-donna bandleader,
a place to lay up or cool out.
Tadd said he wrote better at Mary's.
Monk, in those years, found it hard
to be out in the world.
They came to the Terrace,
she sometimes thought,
because someone
was sending them to her.

Mainly they came to work
in the afternoons or the wee smalls:
Bird or Miles,
Dizzy, the bell of his horn
bent from that mishap
at Snookie's,
Hank Jones, lean and elegant,
Bud Powell, before the cops
put him back in Bellevue.

She and the boys would work
around Mary's upright grand,
for hours, rephrasing standards
in lunatic keys, chords flattened,
tempo any which way,
melody just a premise
honored in the breach.

The music had grown,
Mary knew, since her early days
before the war, in circuit bands
and Midwest ballrooms
but now these kids
were growing it new.
And while she could pull them
along here or there,
trim them up if needed,
mainly she just gave them
use of the hall.

1954

By the time in Paris
and in the middle of a set
when she walked offstage,
Mary had been wrestling
with the angel for some years.

Strange,
you think your vocation
lies one way,
think you are a person
with a special destiny,
and the still small voice says:
Well yes, but not as you imagined.

Back home in New York
faith had already taken up residence
in all the places where music had lived
but Mary knew her faith
must have a foundation and home
in a practice of its own.

Her friends were confused,
her family offended
(Why not the Baptists
like she'd been raised?)
when Mary went
to the Catholics.

To the few to whom she explained,
she explained:
it wasn't because
she owed anything to Rome,
wasn't anything she was trying to say
about her family in Pittsburgh.
It was just that
Our Lady of Lourdes
on 142nd St. between
Convent and Amsterdam,
was the only church

in the neighborhood
that was open all night.

On a Photograph in Life Magazine of Mary Lou Williams Playing in Gjon Mili's Studio, 1943

Even Milt Gabler came down
from his throne at Decca Records
to stand around and get photographed
with the Signal Corps guys
who were putting the whole program
on V-Discs for the troops.

The Conde-Nast people put little tables
around Mili's giant studio.
Vogue models sat
at a number of these,
practicing the art of fetching
while Mili circulated in the crowd
of industry insiders,
shooting everything for *Life*.

Seemed like all the musicians
who weren't in the Army
were in Midtown that fall.
As the nightclubs closed
and the broadcasting studios
went off the air
Alpha and Omega
came up Mili's stairs
to play until 10
the next morning.

Shooting over the shoulder
of Al Lucas and his big double bass,
Mili gets Mary at the keyboard
smiling with a wicked surprise
for somebody.

Life ran the photo across the seam
from a picture of Billie Holliday
singing "Fine and Mellow,"
and over the caption:

112

"Miss Williams, who arranges
for the Duke Ellington Band,
is one of the very few
capable female jazz
musicians."

Mary Lou Williams (Portrait Sitting) by Dennis Stock, Gelatin Silver Print

She was converted to Roman Catholicism in 1954,
a few years before Stock took the picture
at her home on Long Island.
Her faith is evident in the photograph
from the small image of the Annunciation
that stands on the piano where she leans,
elbows on the keyboard behind her,
in a way that puts her breasts directly
at the focal point of the composition.
On her features irritation with the prying,
young, white photographer contends futilely
with the mild forbearance of the Lamb.

Acknowledgements

The authors would like to thank the hard-working and open-minded editors and publishers who have given space and support to our work over the past few years. Some of the poems in this volume have appeared in *Borderlands: Texas Poetry Review, Eastern Iowa Review, The Penn Review, Unbroken, Blue Mountain Review, Misfit Magazine, The Tulane Review, The Westchester Review, Paper Brigade Daily, The Nasonia,* and *They Said: A Multi-Genre Anthology of Contemporary Collaborative Writing* (Black Lawrence Press, 2018).

Further Reading

The authors of this collection have provided a reading list so that readers may take a closer look at the individual lives explored in this collection as well as the genre of speculative biography.

Aronson, Marc and Budhos, Marina. *Eyes of the World: Robert Capa, Gerda Taro, and the Invention of Modern Photojournalism.* Henry Holt, 2017.
Baker, Carlos. *Emerson Among the Eccentrics.* Viking, 1996.
Bloemink, Barbara. *Florine Stettheimer: A Biography.* Hirmer, 2022.
Dahl, Linda. *Morning Glory: A Biography of Mary Lou Williams.* University of California Press, 2001.
Fielding, Vivian Daphne, *The Rainbow Picnic: A Portrait of Iris Tree.* Methuen, 1974.
Manning, Maurice. *Railsplitter.* Copper Canyon Press, 2019.
Pettinger, Peter. *Bill Evans, How My Heart Sings.* Yale University Press, 2002.
Simic, Charles. *Dime-Store Alchemy,* NYRB Classics, 2011.
Warren, Robert Penn. *Audubon: A Vision.* Random House, 1969.
Wert, Jeffrey D.. *General James Longstreet: The Confederacy's Most Controversial Soldier.* Simon and Schuster, 1993.
Whelan, Richard. *Robert Capa: A Biography.* University of Nebraska Press, 1994.

About the Authors

Mark Luebbers has been an English teacher and administrator at several schools in the Northeast and Midwest. He now lives in Greenfield, Massachusetts. His poems have been included in recent issues of *The American Journal of Poetry*, *Apple Valley Review, Blue Line, The Hopper, Salt Front, The Wayfarer Magazine*, and *Wilderness House Review*. His collection *Flat Light* was published by Urban Farmhouse Press in 2020.

Benjamin Goluboff teaches at Lake Forest College. In addition to some scholarly publications, he has placed imaginative writing — poetry, fiction, and essays — in many small-press journals, recently *Unbroken, Cordite Poetry Review*, and *War Literature and the Arts*. He is the author of *Ho Chi Minh: A Speculative Life in Verse* (Urban Farmhouse Press 2017).

Printed in the USA
CPSIA information can be obtained
at www.ICGtesting.com
LVHW101303140823
754932LV00013B/1180